Felting for Baby

Felting for Baby

25 Warm & Woolly Projects for the Little Ones in Your Life

Saori Yamazaki

TRUMPETER
Boston & London
2009

Contents

· · · · · · · · · · · · ·

A Note on Safety: The items in this book are made with safety in mind, but in some cases, the fabric may unravel or the surface may come off if it is not sufficiently felted. Any items that your child touches should be made carefully and for strength, and you should take care when your child wears or uses them.

· · · · · · · · · · · · ·

Introduction

Felt work involves taking fluffy wool fibers and working with them until the fabric is just the way you like. The items you can make vary widely, and there's no limit to what you can do with your ideas: making cute accessories, practical bags, and items for every day life.

Making something by hand for someone else is a lot of fun, but a special joy is found in making something for a tiny, tiny baby. For example, if you're making booties, you can't help thinking of the cute little feet that you are making them for, and you find yourself smiling. A regular population explosion has been happening among my friends in recent years, and even though I enjoy buying baby gifts in a store, most of the time, my friends expect something handmade. At times like that, I get excited about making something.

I'm confident that my friends are pleased with the warmth of fine handmade felt items. I'd like all of you to try your hand at making felt items, too, whether for an infant, for someone else, or even for yourself.

—SAORI YAMAZAKI

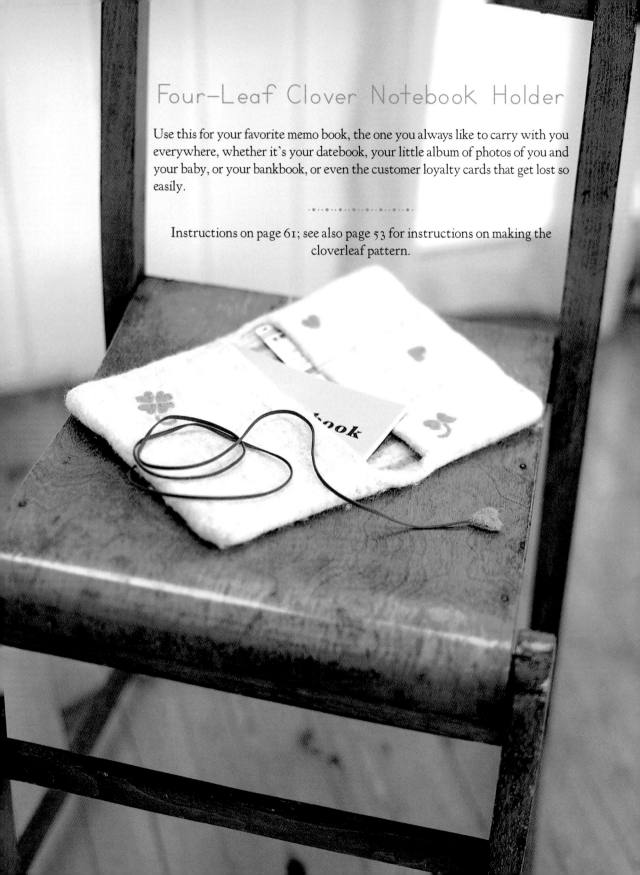

Four-Leaf Clover Notebook Holder

Use this for your favorite memo book, the one you always like to carry with you everywhere, whether it's your datebook, your little album of photos of you and your baby, or your bankbook, or even the customer loyalty cards that get lost so easily.

· · · · · · · · · · · · · · · ·

Instructions on page 61; see also page 53 for instructions on making the cloverleaf pattern.

Warm Vest

Keep this simple vest on hand to put on your baby on those mornings when your house is plagued by chilly drafts or when you go outside. To make this vest, you start with a square and cut out the neckline and armholes, so you can make this vest quickly and easily.

Instructions on page 62.

Gingerbread Man Puppets

These charming puppets come to life when you put your hands inside them. You can use them as cheerful characters to wake your child up in the morning or amuse your child by having the puppets act out stories.

Instructions on page 63.

Felt Basket

This fully formed basket is suitable for holding candy or odds and ends. You can also use it for decorative purposes and fill it with arrangements of dried flowers or fragrant herbs. It immediately adds a touch of elegance to any table.

· · · · · · · · · · · · · ·

Instructions on page 64.

Lamb Place Mat and Coasters

This set is perfect for breakfast or lunch. Just wash and iron the pieces after use, and you'll be able to use them for years. They're so easy to make that you may as well make several place settings.

· ● ·· ● · ● ·· ● · ● ·· ● ·· ● ·

Instructions on page 65.

Flower Garden Magnets

You can make these items with just one needle. Use them to post memos about important appointments or your favorite photos. These magnets make for a charming display that draws your attention to things you need to remember.

· · * · · * · · * · · * · · * · · * · ·

Instructions on page 66; see also page 55 for instructions on making a similar item.

Matching Minibags

These small bags are perfect for when you're going out for just a little while. Adjust the cord as you like: you can make the length suitable for either a child or an adult, or if you make the cord really short, you can have a handbag. If you don't attach a cord at all, the bag serves as a simple pouch.

Instructions on page 67. See also page 48 for more detailed instructions.

Baby Booties

Put these adorable little slippers on your baby's feet for warmth inside a drafty house. Use your imagination and decorate them with pom-poms or other accessories.

・◆・・◆・・◆・・◆・・◆・・◆・

Instructions on page 69.

Mama's Bag

You can use this practical, roomy bag to hold everything for baby. It's so lightweight and easy to carry that you'll want to carry it every day. The bag's distinguishing feature is the flower pattern, while the background of natural colored wool gives it a quietly mature feel.

• • • • • • • • • • • • • •

Instructions on page 68.

Baby's Backpack

Fill this little backpack with snacks, tissues, or other necessities, and you'll be ready for anything when you take your child out. Adjust the length of the straps to your child's size so that you can easily put it on and take it off.

· • · • · • · • · • · • · • ·

Instructions on page 71.

Clatter Balls

These balls click softly when you roll them.
You start with a plastic bell and enclose it
in felt, finishing the whole thing off with
heart-shaped stitching.

· * · · * · · * · * · · * · * · *

Instructions on page 72.

Pastel—Colored Play Mat

This mat can be the center of your child's playroom. If the floor is slippery, you can attach anti-skid tape to the underside. It's warm and fluffy, and the right size for adults to use as a lap blanket.

· ● · · ● · · ● · · ● · · ● · · ● · · ● ·

Instructions on page 73.

Soft Flower Vase

Wrapping an ordinary glass flower vase in felt gives it a distinctive and contemporary feel. After all, green goes well with wool, which comes from sheep that graze in green meadows. And with its felt covering, this vase won't break if it falls over.

Instructions on page 74.

Polka Dot Hangers

Show off your children's clothing in a more attractive way with a soft and fluffy hanger. With its rounded ends, a felted hanger is perfect for lightweight shirts. It also adds an elegant, decorative touch to your child's room.

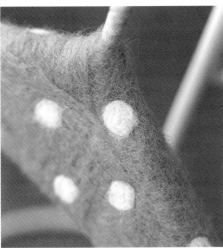

· ◆ · · ◆ · · ◆ · · ◆ · · ◆ · · ◆ ·

Instructions on page 75.

Elf Hat

Seeing your child in this hat will bring a smile to everyone's face, as it conjures up an image of a mischievous elf right out of a fairy tale. This hat covers the ears for extra warmth and is lined with soft merino wool.

• • • • • • • • • • • • •

Instructions on page 76.

Felt Ball Hair Tie

All you have to do to make this sweet accessory is take round balls of felt and attach them to an elastic hair tie. You can make them in several colors, so that you and your daughter can choose the ones that match your outfits.

· · · · · · · · · · · · · · · · ·

Instructions on page 77.

Wall Pockets

Make a large felt sheet and then add as many pockets and photo frames as you like to create an item that serves as both storage and decoration. Hang it by your child's bed to store toys and storybooks.

Instructions on page 78.

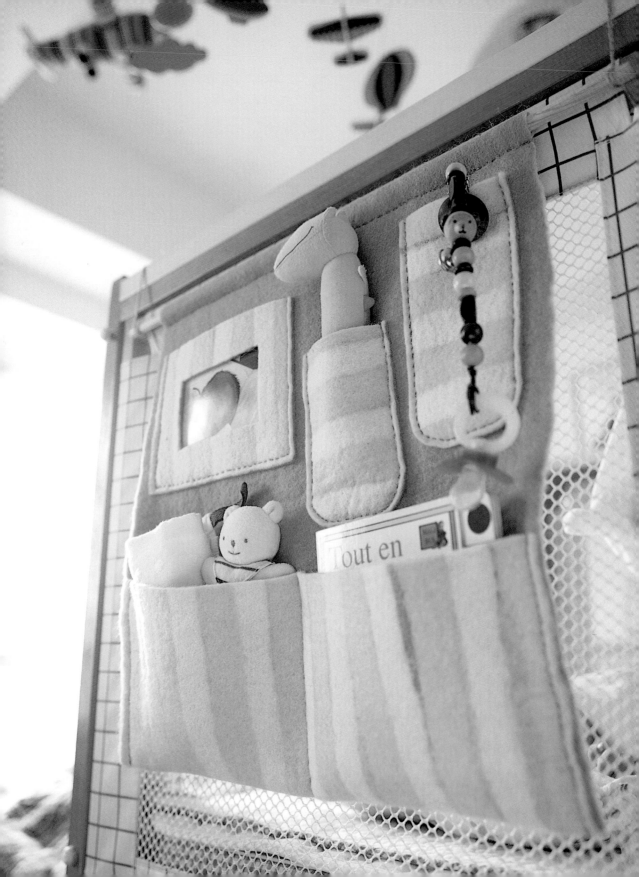

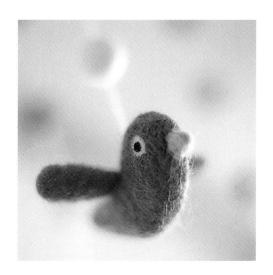

Bluebird Mobile

These bluebirds bring true happiness and sweet dreams to your home as they fly through the air. They keep flying after just a gentle push, lulling your child into a peaceful afternoon nap.

· · * · · * · · * · · * · · * · · * · ·

Instructions on page 80.

Mini Cushions

These mini cushions have more uses than you might imagine. Lay them under your head for a quick nap, or lean on them when taking a break from deskwork, or use them in any situation that suits your fancy.

Instructions on page 82.

Fragrant Sachets

If you're making something that keeps the air fresh, it's best to use natural ingredients. Fill these sachets with dried herbs, and they will give off a faint fragrance.

.*.*.*.*.*.*.*.

Instructions on page 84.

Mushroom Box

This mushroom-shaped container will have a subtle presence in any room.

· • · · • · • · • · • · • · · • ·

Instructions on page 85.

Baby Bottle Holder

The handles make this holder easy to carry anywhere. The heat retaining properties of wool make it possible for the contents to stay warm for quite a long time. You can use this holder to carry not only baby bottles, but also other containers for hot beverages.

Instructions on page 86.

Teddy Bear

With its steady stare, this teddy bear is un-
like any other and will touch the heart of
your child.

·.·.·.·.·.·.·.·.·.·.·.·.

Instructions on page 88.

How to Felt

The basic principle behind felt work is taking fluffy, raw wool fibers and intertwining them to create a stable form. This process is the act of felting. The two main types are wet felting and needle felting. The choice of which technique you use depends on the project.

Step-by-step instructions of each technique are explained on the following pages. While making the projects in this book, refer to these instructions to help you master the basic techniques and special tricks.

Wet Felting

In this technique, you take a small amount of liquid detergent, add it to hot water (this mixture is referred to simply as hot, soapy water in this book), moisten the wool fibers with it, and push and rub the fibers into shape. The chemical properties and heat of the liquid detergent, and the vibration and friction from your hands, cause the wool fibers to entwine and mat evenly, resulting in a smooth, strong fabric. This efficient technique is appropriate for making sheets of felt or felt with a lot of volume.

Needle Felting

In this technique, you use a specially designed felting needle (which I will refer to simply as a needle) to poke a series of holes in the fabric. The wool fibers become entangled in the small irregularities made by the needle and entwine with one another to create a felt surface. All you need for this process is one needle. This technique is especially convenient for making small items, detailed patterns, and three-dimensional shapes.

Dividing the Wool

The main type of wool used in this book is known as roving, which is raw wool that has been cleaned, carded, and gathered into long strips. (In this book, I will simply refer to roving as "wool.") You can divide the roving into the amount you need using the method shown below.

Center your hands on the point where you want to divide the wool and then move them about 4" away from that spot in both directions.

Tug sharply from both ends to divide the wool. Don't pull too hard, and move your hands horizontally.

How not to do it: the wool will not separate if you have your hands too close together or if you pull too hard.

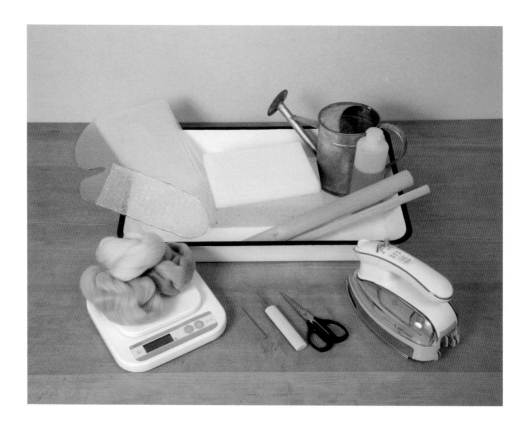

The Main Tools

For Wet Felting

Shallow Basin: A shallow basin or container of some kind is useful when making a sheet of felt as it helps to contain the water used in the felting process. Alternately, you can use the kitchen sink.

Hot, Soapy Water: Add 3 or 4 drops of dishwashing detergent to about 1 quart of hot water. Adjust the amount so that it will foam slightly when you apply it to the wool, and rub. The hotter the water is, the faster the felting process will occur. Lukewarm or cold water takes more time.

Watering Can: Use this to sprinkle the carded wool lightly with hot, soapy water

so that it doesn't separate. A spray bottle also works.

Bubble Wrap: Use this when making flat items. Cut a piece of bubble wrap the same size as your project. Lay the wet felt out and roll it up together with the wool during the felting process. You can also use plastic sheeting.

Waterproof Pattern Paper: Make patterns for your projects from a material that will not lose its shape when wet. Plastic sheeting and bubble wrap work well, but you can use the coated cardboard from milk cartons, too.

Wooden Dowel: You can advance the felting process by wrapping the wool around a wooden dowel or rolling pin. The larger your project is, the thicker the rolling pin should be.

Plastic Bags: When you're rubbing and pressing the wool, placing plastic bags on your hands will reduce friction.

Digital Scale: This measures wool correctly in ounces.

Scissors: Well-sharpened scissors are helpful when cutting through thick felt.

Iron: Use an iron to smooth out the work and dry it at the same time.

For Needle Felting

Felting Needle: This special needle has barbs at the end that help to grab the wool. Felting needles come in many sizes. If you are working on a large surface, use the kind that has several needles embedded in a handle.

Sponge: Look for sponges that are made especially for felting.

For All Projects

In some cases, you may need sewing needles, thread, or towels (as pressing cloths) in addition to the tools described here.

Lessons in Wet Felting ◉

Lesson 1: How to Make a Sheet of Felt with a Pattern

Divide the wool into strands of equal length, and lay them parallel to one another for the time being. You can make felt sheets of as many layers as you wish. These photographs illustrate the process of making a rectangle, 5⅞" by 8⅝", that is five layers thick with contrasting, decorative felt circles. At the same time, you will learn how to add felted shapes.

1. Divide the Wool

Measure out ½ ounce of wool, and fold it into five equal lengths. Separate the segments as shown on page 41 to make five equal strands. Prepare a small amount of contrasting wool for the circles.

2. Lay the Wool Horizontally (Layer 1)

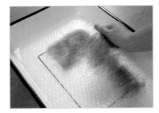

Draw a rectangle 6⅝" x 9⅞" (or 15% to 20% larger than the finished size) on a piece of bubble wrap. Then take one strand of wool, pull off small amounts, and line up the individual fibers horizontally. Spread them out evenly so that the entire rectangle is covered to the edges.

3. Lay the Wool Vertically (Layer 2)

Take the second strand of wool, pull it apart, and lay the fibers on top of the first layer. The first layer was placed horizontally, so lay the second layer vertically. When you're making a sheet of felt, be sure to alternate between placing the wool horizontally and vertically so that no two layers are placed in the same direction.

4. Repeat for Five Layers

Now move on to the third layer, and lay the wool fibers out horizontally. Lay the fourth layer vertically, and the fifth horizontally again. Because the fibers entwine with one another in a complex manner during felting, good technique requires shredding the wool finely and laying the fibers out in a perfectly regular pattern.

5. Start Felting

Use a watering can to sprinkle the wool lightly with hot, soapy water. To ensure that the layers don't lose their shape, hold them gently in place as you wet them. The moistened fibers will start matting together, initiating the felting process.

6. Gently Press the Liquid into the Wool

Wear plastic bags over your hands to prevent friction, and gently work the detergent through the wool. Taking care not to destroy the shape of the wool layers, press and rub the surface lightly to expel any air trapped among the fibers.

7. Adjust the Shape and Thickness

When you have worked the detergent through all the wool, straighten the four sides, using the rectangle as a guide. Since it's easy to end up with thinner, weaker edges, take care to ensure that the entire sheet is of a uniform thickness.

8. Create the Felted Shapes

Dampen the contrasting wool with hot, soapy water, and form it into the desired shape while stretching it out horizontally with your hands. Once you lay it out on the felt sheet, you will find it difficult to modify, so be sure to work the contrasting wool gently into the desired shape at this stage.

9. Continue Felting

Lay the contrasting pieces where you want them on the felt sheet, and gently work them in. Add more detergent as you lightly stroke and rub in the contrasting fibers with even circular motions, starting with light strokes and gradually increasing pressure.

10. Roll the Felt

Once the surface has become matted together, roll the felt up in the bubble wrap. Make sure that you don't leave any gaps or distortions. Roll the bubble wrap from the bottom up. To ensure that the shapes stay in place, start pressing lightly, gradually increasing the pressure across the whole surface. Unroll the sheet, and smooth out the wrinkles.

11. Roll the Felt from All Sides

Roll the sheet up again, first from the top, then from the left and right. Turn the sheet over, and repeat the process of rolling it from all four edges. If the felt dries out, sprinkle more hot, soapy water on it. If you are creating a sheet of felt, roll it up a total of eight times from different edges and both front and back.

12. Roll the Sheet with the Dowel

Remove the bubble wrap, and roll the felt sheet up with a wooden dowel. As before, roll it up from all four edges on both sides. Each time you unroll it, smooth out the wrinkles; add more hot, soapy water if the piece dries out. Repeat the process until the sheet has shrunk to its finished size and proper shape.

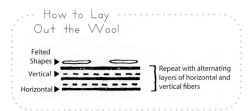

How to Lay Out the Wool

Felted Shapes ▶
Vertical ▶
Horizontal ▶

] Repeat with alternating layers of horizontal and vertical fibers

13. Trim the Edges

If you want straight edges, cut them while they're still wet and work them into shape. If you want a more natural, fluffy look, leave the edges untrimmed.

14. Finishing

Rinse the finished sheet in lukewarm water, then put it through the spin cycle in the washing machine to remove any excess water. Smooth the surface with an iron.

15. The Finished Felt Sheet

The completed, patterned felt sheet after natural air drying.

Wool Felt Sheets

Sheets of 100% wool felt are a popular craft item. A wool felt sheet is a fluffy sheet of felt with the fibers so closely entwined that the piece is like a blanket. To make a shaped item on a sheet of felt, you don't have to go through steps 1 through 4 of dividing and arranging the wool. All you have to do to incorporate even a small shape is cut it out of a contrasting piece of wool felt and work it in as with regular wet felting.

1. Cut the background pieces from a sheet of wool felt. Cut the shape slightly larger than the desired finished measurements, and layer the pieces as thickly as desired.

2. Moisten the felt sheets with hot, soapy water, work it in gently, and then place a contrasting piece of felt cut into a shape on top.

3. Incorporate the shape into the felt sheet by going through steps 5 to 14 of the wet felting process.

4. Let the wool dry naturally and you're all done, without any distortions in the pattern or irregularities in the surface. (Note: The appropriate size and thickness of the felt sheet will vary depending on the specific project. Make adjustments accordingly.)

Lesson 2: How to Make Bag-Shaped and Three-Dimensional Forms

This technique is appropriate for making objects such as bags, storage pockets, or slippers. It is an adaptation of the technique for making sheets, but here you wrap the wool fibers around pattern paper as you felt. This series of photographs shows how to make the bodies of the Matching Minibags shown on page 17. The pattern appears on page 67.

1. Arrange Side A

Take about 1 ounce of wool and divide it into eight equal strands as shown on page 41. Make two layers, one horizontal and one vertical, on the pattern paper, using one strand of wool per layer. Even out the area, and spread out the wool so that it's a bit larger than the pattern area. (I refer to the front of the bag as side A and the back as side B.) Apply hot, soapy water to the two layers of wool and work it in thoroughly with your hands.

2. Work Side A

Turn the whole project over, along with the pattern paper. (If the piece is large, remove the pattern paper before turning it over and then replace it on the new top side.) If any of the fibers are sticking out, fold them over the pattern paper and work the edges and corners thoroughly.

3. Arrange Side B

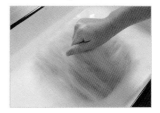

Make two layers, one horizontal and one vertical, on another piece of pattern paper, using one strand of wool per layer. Then place side B on top of side A, pattern papers together.

4. Work Side B

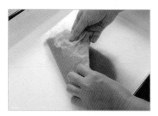

Work the surface of side B with hot, soapy water, then turn the whole project over again. Turn it gently to make sure that the part you worked doesn't come apart or tear away.

5. Make a Bag Shape

As in step 2, fold over any wool fibers that stick out. Repeat steps 1 through 4 on both sides so that both sides have four layers of wool each.

6. Continue Felting

Put plastic bags over both hands, and start rubbing the felt in circular motions around the center, first gently, and then with more force. You can increase the pressure by pressing with the very tips of your fingers. Be sure to work the edges and corners thoroughly.

The process of arranging and dampening the wool is the same as the one shown on pages 45 and 46. Refer back to those pages if you're not sure how to proceed.

Placement of Wool and Pattern Paper

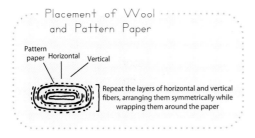

Pattern paper   Horizontal   Vertical

Repeat the layers of horizontal and vertical fibers, arranging them symmetrically while wrapping them around the paper

7. Pinch Test

Pinch a bit of the surface to see whether the fibers are firmly intertwined. (Be sure to check both side A and side B.) If the fibers come lose or break off, then the felting process is incomplete; repeat step 6.

8. Cut an Opening

Use scissors to cut an opening on the side that will be the mouth of the bag. (You'll felt the cut in step 11 to strengthen it.)

9. Remove the Pattern Paper

Slide the pattern papers out. Because the felting process is not yet complete on the inside of the bag, hold the bag carefully so that the insides don't stick to each other.

10. Turn It Right Side Out

Turn the bag right side out, taking care not to tear or stretch any of the felted fibers.

11. Felt the Edges and Opening

Flatten out the side edges of the bag and carefully rub and work them so that they felt. Since the opening cut in step 8 may be weak, work it for a while so that it's straight and sturdy.

12. Roll Up All Sides from Four Directions

Use a wooden dowel to roll up both side A and side B from the top, bottom, right, and left. Each time you unroll the felt, smooth out the wrinkles. If it starts to dry out, apply a little more hot, soapy water. Repeat this step until the whole piece has shrunk evenly and to the desired dimensions.

13. Shape the Bottom

Fold the bottom so that it's like a paper grocery bag, and rub and work it to form and stabilize the shape. Do the same with both side A and side B.

14. Make It Three-Dimensional

Stand the bag up, insert your hand, and flatten the inside bottom. Consider the proportions of the entire bag as you carefully felt the interior sides, angles, and opening, so that no distorted or uneven surfaces remain.

15. Adjust the Opening

Adjust the opening so that the bag is a uniform height. Apply some more hot, soapy water to the cut edges of the opening and work it in.

16. Stabilize the Shape

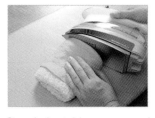

Rinse the bag in lukewarm water and briefly run it through the spin cycle of a washing machine. Stabilize the shape by ironing it, using a towel to keep the bag's shape.

17. Finishing

Let the felt dry naturally, and you will end up with the main body of a bag.

18. The Finished Bag

The bag is ready for any finishing touches. Attach a zipper and shoulder strap to the finished bag, as you like. (See page 67 for the full instructions for the Matching Minibags.)

Lesson 3: How to Wrap a Core

You can use something other than wool as the core for forming your work. This technique makes easy, long-lasting, and pretty silhouettes. Here's how to make the Clatter Balls on page 24.

1. Wrap the Wool around a Core

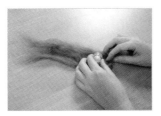

Prepare ³/₄ ounces of wool. Take a small amount, and wrap it entirely around the plastic bell (the core of this item).

2. Start Felting

Take the wrapped bell, and soak it in hot, soapy water until the wool is thoroughly moistened. Then start working the detergent gently into the wool.

3. Add More Wool

Wrap the remaining wool around the bell little by little, making sure to leave no gaps and varying the direction from which you start, until the bell is wrapped to a uniform thickness.

4. Continue Felting

Put the fully wrapped bell into a plastic bag and form the item into something the size of a tennis ball. Make it as round as possible by directing the pressure to the center.

5. Add a Shape

Cut a shape out of a sheet of felt and work it into the item, following the instructions on page 47.

6. The Finished Ball

Rinse the item with lukewarm water and briefly run it through the spin cycle of a washing machine to remove any excess water. Once the item has dried naturally, finish it by hand stitching around the pattern.

Lessons in Needle Felting

Lesson 1: How to Make Shapes

Use a felting needle to create a decorative shape by attaching wool to previously felted material. These photographs show you how to attach a cloverleaf design to a sheet of felt.

1. Arrange the Wool

Place a small amount of wool on the spot where you want to make a design, and gently shape the edges with a needle.

2. Set the Design

Carefully set the entire design by poking it into the felt. If you want to have an allover design, poke the entire surface of the design, leaving no irregularities.

3. The Finished Pattern

Finish the pattern by adding additional leaves and a stalk. You may also add decorative stitching.

The Underside of the Sheet

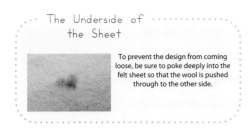

To prevent the design from coming loose, be sure to poke deeply into the felt sheet so that the wool is pushed through to the other side.

Lesson 2: How to Make Three-Dimensional Items

You can make three-dimensional items with nothing more than a felting needle and a handful of wool. You can form objects with a needle or attach them to one another.

Felt Ball

1. Roll the Wool into a Ball

Roll a small amount of wool into a ball. Make it as compact and tight as possible, as if forming a core.

2. Poke It into Shape

Poke it into shape with a needle. Roll it around as you refine its shape; reinforce places that seem loose with more wool.

3. The Finished Ball

Keep adding small amounts of wool and poking it into shape until the ball reaches the desired size.

Flower

1. Make the Center

Use a needle to make a ball of wool; flatten the ball slightly while adjusting the shape with the needle.

2. Round the Top

Poke at it from the sides to raise the top a bit, while flattening the underside.

3. Make the Flower Petals

Use your needle to make a flattened, oval-shaped clump of wool. Leave part of it fluffy.

Sometimes you don't need to use a needle and can just form items by hand. Roll pieces of felt like a meatball, and smooth them with your fingertips.

4. Attach a Petal

Attach the fluffy part of the petals to the center using the needle. Almost all needle-felted parts can be attached to one another by this method.

5. Attach All the Petals

Attach as many petals as you wish. Attach them with the needle by layering the fluffy ends.

6. The Finished Flower

Finish the surface and gaps with a needle to complete the project.

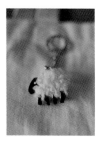

Felt Q&A: Helpful Hints

Q: I'm in the midst of a project, and I'm not sure how to proceed with laying out the felt.

A: Remember to alternate horizontal and vertical layers. Also, you can't go wrong if you remember to start with a horizontal layer.

Q: My wet felting projects don't shrink to the size that I want, and on the whole, they seem loose.

A: Repeat the felting process, using pages 45 to 47 for reference. If you use the wool and pattern paper described in the instruction pages of these books correctly, you'll end up with an item of the correct size.

Q: I finished a bag, but the area around the corners seems thin.

A: Add more of the same kind of wool on the wrong side, and poke it with a needle to reinforce it. If any stray threads are visible on the outside, poke them through to the inside. Apply some detergent to the area for a more natural feel.

Q: The edges of the sheets tend to fray.

A: Carefully control the thickness during the felting stage, and continue felting after you have cut and assembled the sheets.

Q: My needle felting projects don't seem to have enough volume.

A: Adjust this by adding a bit more wool to the areas that seem thin and poking it through.

Q: Parts of my needle felting projects come apart.

A: Use the needle again to reinforce them. If they are not thoroughly attached, use an appropriate amount of the same wool to strengthen them.

Q: My attempts to make designs with a needle never turn out right.

A: It may be helpful to draw the design with a marking pencil. After that, be sure to attach small amounts of wool bit by bit. If you end up adding too much wool, gently remove it.

It's easy to make felt projects if you learn the patterns!

When you make your first felt pieces, you'll hesitate and fumble, but these patterns are simple and uniform. When you look at the instructions for an item, you'll find it easier to work on if you can envision the finished product. One characteristic of felt work is that it's easy to reinforce and repair your items with a needle. Don't give up if you make a mistake, large or small. Just repeat the procedures or repair the item carefully, and you'll end up with an item that you can show or give to others with pride.

How to Make the Projects

About the Instructions

* The ⨍ symbol indicates needle felting, while the ⬩ symbol indicates wet felting.
* Be sure to look at page 42 for a list of the tools you will need to have on hand.
* The pattern pieces and plans for the items are found together on pages 89 to 92.
* Depending on how well the needle felting process goes, the specified amount of wool may not be sufficient. I recommend that beginners prepare a bit more than the specified amount of wool.
* In these instructions, the word "needle" refers to a felting needle, but when hand stitching, use either an embroidery needle or a sewing needle.
* If you don't understand the details of the following instructions, refer to the photographic explanations on pages 45 to 55.

Four-Leaf Clover Notebook Holder

Photograph on page 8.

Photograph on page 8.

Finished Size: 7 ⅛″ × 11″

Note: The method for embedding the decoration is described in the photographic series on page 53.

Materials

* Wool for the main body: Beige, 2½ ounces
* Wool for the stripes and patterns: Green, less than ¼ ounce
* Suede cord: 35½"

Instructions

1. Divide the wool for the body of the case into eight equal parts.
2. Cut out a piece of pattern paper 12½" × 9". Working from the inside to the outside, felt four layers of wool on both sides of the pattern paper to make a bag shape: first lay the green stripes on the paper, then lay out the beige layers to be felted.
3. Cut an opening down the center of one side, remove the pattern paper, and turn the case right side out. Continue felting the case, rolling it up from all sides until it is the size of the pattern. Using the template on page 91, cut away the opening of the pocket at right angles and work it carefully.
4. Rinse and spin dry the case, iron it, and let it dry thoroughly.
5. Sew the right side in two places, dividing it into three pockets.
6. Attach the cord and embed the decoration in the front. It's finished when you have embedded the clover pattern (page 91).

Steps 2 and 3

Make sure the green stripes are aligned and embedded in the beige felt before you finish the felting in Step 3.

Center

Steps 3 to 6

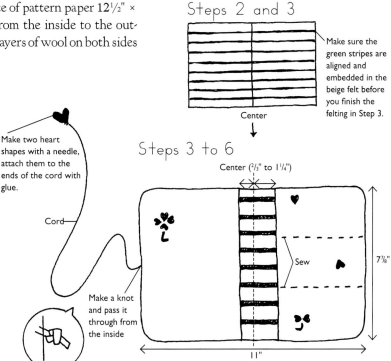

Make two heart shapes with a needle, attach them to the ends of the cord with glue.

Cord

Make a knot and pass it through from the inside

Center (⅔" to 1¼")

Sew

7⅞"

11"

Warm Vest ○

Photograph on page 10.

Finished Size: 10½″ long, chest measurement 22″

Note: The method for making a bag shape is shown on pages 48 to 49.

Materials

* Wool for the outside: Natural, 1¾ ounces
* Wool for the inside: Orange, 1¾ ounces
* Four wooden buttons: ½″ in diameter

Instructions

1. Divide the wool for both the inside and the lining into four parts each.

2. Cut out a piece of pattern paper 13⅜″ × 16″ (see page 91). Working from the outside to the inside, felt four layers of wool on both sides of the pattern paper to make a bag shape: felt two layers of the natural wool for the outside, then two layers of orange wool for the inside.

3. Cut an opening along the bottom, remove the pattern paper, and turn the vest right side out. Roll the vest, felting it until it is the size indicated in the diagram. Cut the collar and armholes and work them so that they felt.

4. Rinse and spin the vest, iron it, and let it dry thoroughly.

5. Attach the buttons to both shoulders, and cut corresponding buttonholes.

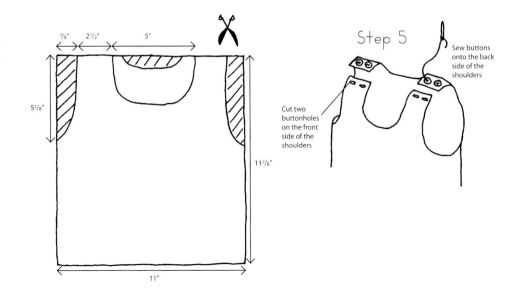

Gingerbread Man Puppets

Photograph on pages 12–13.

Finished Size: 5 1/2″ x 9 1/2″

Finished Size: 5 1/2″ x 9 1/2″

Note: The method for making a bag shape is shown on pages 48 to 49.

Materials

* Wool for the main body: Natural or camel, 1 ounce
* Wool for the face and buttons: Brown, small amounts

Instructions

1. Divide the wool for the main body into eight parts
2. Cut out a piece of pattern paper (see page 91). Felt four layers of wool on both sides of the pattern paper to make a bag shape.
3. Cut an opening across the bottom, remove the pattern paper, and turn the puppet right side out. (Carefully use a rod to turn the arms and neck inside out.) Felt the puppet by rolling it up from all sides until it reaches the size indicated in the diagram.
4. Rinse and spin the puppet, iron it, and let it dry naturally.
5. Put a sponge inside the puppet and use a needle to felt the face and buttons onto the puppet.

When you arrange the wool and wrap it, use scissors to cut the parts with the small gaps to help shape the puppet

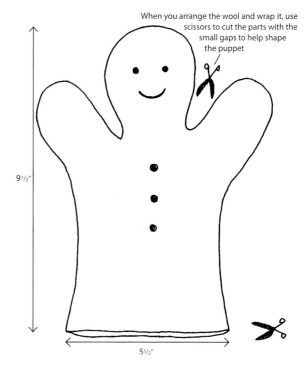

9 1/2″

5 1/2″

Felt Basket

Photograph on page 14.

Finished Size: 11" x 9⅞" following the curve of the basket

Materials

* Wool for the main body: Beige, 1¾ ounces
* Leather strap: 1" × 11⅞"

Instructions

1. Divide the wool for the basket into six parts.

2. Make a circular felt sheet of six layers on pattern paper (see page 89, or draw a perfect circle 12½" in diameter).

3. When the circle has been fairly well felted, raise the sides to make it three dimensional and continue felting until it's the size indicated in the diagram. Placing the basket in another container may help to shape the sides.

4. Make sure that the sides are a uniform height and that the edges are smooth.

5. Rinse and spin the basket, iron it, and let it dry naturally.

6. Attach the leather strap.

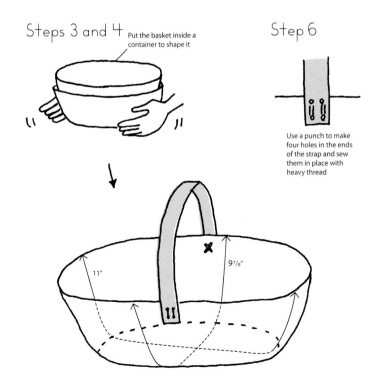

Steps 3 and 4 Put the basket inside a container to shape it

Step 6

Use a punch to make four holes in the ends of the strap and sew them in place with heavy thread

11"

9⅞"

Lamb Place Mat and Coasters

Photograph on page 15.

Finished Size: Coaster, 4 1/2"
square; Place Mat, 12 1/2" x 9"

Materials (for one mat and
two coasters)

* Wool felt sheet for the main body:
  Beige, 19 3/4" × 39 3/8"
* Wool felt sheet for the pattern: Gray,
  9 7/8" × 19 3/4"

Instructions

1. Cut the larger sheet of beige felt into
   four pieces 9 7/8" × 19 3/4" each. Then cut
   each of these pieces into one piece 9 7/8"
   × 13 3/4" and two squares 4 7/8".

2. Create templates of the patterns found
   on page 90. Cut one piece for the face,
   two for the ears, and eight for the foot-
   prints from the contrasting sheet of felt.

3. Stack the four large beige pieces together. Make two stacks of four pieces
   each from the smaller beige squares.
   Place the shapes on top of the stacks
   as shown in the diagram. Apply hot,
   soapy water to each stack and work it
   in gently.

4. Felt each stack until it becomes one felted
   sheet. Once the pattern is thoroughly
   worked in, rub and roll the pieces, con-
   tinuing to felt them until they reach the
   size indicated in the diagram.

5. Cut around the pieces as shown in the
   diagram, and work the edges to smooth
   them. Rinse, spin, and iron the pieces,
   and then let them dry naturally.

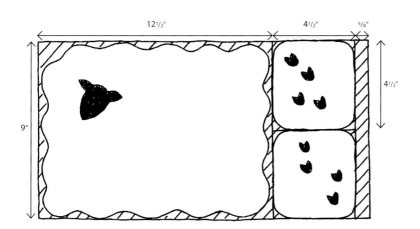

Flower Garden Magnets ⓡ

Photograph on page 16.

Finished Size: Honeybee, about ⅝″ tall x ⅞″ wide x 1⅝″ long; Flower, about ⅜″ tall x 1¾″ in diameter

Note: Instructions for a similar item are found in the photographs on page 54.

Materials for the Honeybee

* Wool for the body: Yellow, about ¾ ounce
* Wool for the wings: White, a small amount
* Wool for the head and stripes: Black, a small amount
* Magnet: ¾" in diameter

Materials for the Flower

* Wool for the petals: Light blue or pink, about ¾ ounce

* Wool for the center: White, a small amount
* Magnet: ¾" in diameter

Instructions for the Honeybee

1. Following the directions on page 54 on How to Make a Flower and referring to the dimensions in the diagram, make the body of the honeybee.

Instructions for the Flower

1. Following the directions on page 54 on How to Make a Flower and referring to the dimensions in the diagram, make eight flower petals and one central piece.
2. Needle felt the petals onto the central piece in the order shown in the diagram.
3. Attach the magnet with glue.

Flower Petal

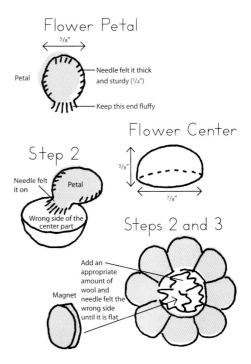

Honeybee

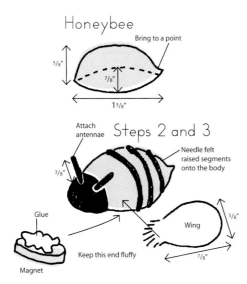

Matching Minibags ◑ ⓕ

Photograph on page 17.

Finished Size: 4″ wide × 4″ tall × 2⅜″ deep

Note: The procedure for making these bags is shown in the photographs on pages 48 to 49.

Materials

* Wool for the bag: Chartreuse, 1 ounce
* Wool for the felt ball: Yellow, a small amount
* One zipper: 4¾" long
* Leather cord: ⅛" × 39⅜" to 43¼" for a child or 59⅛" to 63" for an adult

Instructions

1. Divide the wool for the main body of the bag into eight equal parts.

2. Cut out a piece of pattern paper (see page 92). Felt four layers of wool on both sides of the pattern paper to make a bag shape.

3. Cut an opening across the mouth of the bag, remove the pattern paper, and turn the bag right side out. Continue felting by rolling and unrolling the bag from all sides.

4. Make the bottom of the bag by felting it into a three-dimensional shape. Referring to the dimensions in the diagram, work around the mouth of the bag to ensure a uniform height.

5. Rinse, spin, and iron the bag, and then let it dry naturally.

6. Sew the zipper into the mouth of the bag by hand or by machine. Use a needle to make a felt ball, and tie it on the zipper pull with thread.

7. Cut holes on the sides of the bag through which to pass the leather cord. If they're small enough, you won't have to worry about the cord coming out.

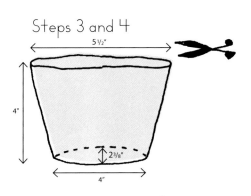

Steps 3 and 4

5½"

4"

2⅜"

4"

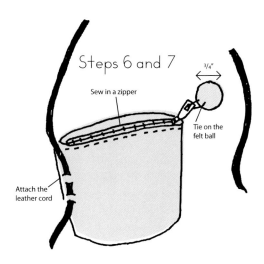

Steps 6 and 7

Sew in a zipper

Attach the leather cord

¾"

Tie on the felt ball

Mama's Bag

Photograph on pages 20–21.

Finished Size: 5³⁄₈" wide
x 13³⁄₈" tall x 3¹⁄₈" deep

Materials

* Wool for the outside of the bag: Natural, 3¹⁄₂ ounces
* Wool for the inside of the bag: Camel, 3¹⁄₂ ounces
* Wool felt sheets for the patterns: Camel and Brown, 1 piece each, 9⁷⁄₈" × 19³⁄₄"
* Wool felt sheet for the handle: Brown, 9⁷⁄₈" × 19³⁄₄"

Instructions

1. Divide the wool for the inside and outside into six equal parts each.
2. Create templates of the patterns found on page 90. Cut the patterns from the felt sheets: 7 large pieces and 5 small pieces from each color for a total of 24 pieces. Cut out the center for each flower, and put it in the center of a flower of the contrasting color.
3. Cut a piece of pattern paper into a rectangle 17³⁄₄" × 15³⁄₄" (see page 90). Working from the outside to the inside, felt six layers of wool on both sides of the pattern paper to make a bag shape: first arrange the flowers on the paper, then felt three layers of natural wool for the outside, then felt three layers of camel wool for the inside.
4. Cut an opening across the mouth of the bag, and remove the pattern paper.
5. Continue the felting process by rolling and unrolling the bag from all sides until it reaches the desired size. Also work around the mouth so that the bag has a uniform height.
6. Rinse, spin, and iron the bag, and then let it dry naturally.
7. With the bag inside out, form gussets by flattening the bottom corners of the bag to a width of 3¹⁄₈". Sew across the bottom of the gusset, fold the corners up, and sew them in place.
8. Cut the felt sheet for the handle into two pieces, 9⁷⁄₈" × 9⁷⁄₈". Roll up each piece tightly from one end, apply hot, soapy water, then roll and rub each until it is 15³⁄₄" long. Sew the ends of each handle to the bag as shown.

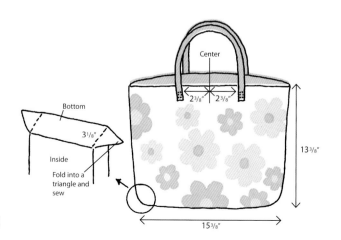

Center

2³⁄₈" 2³⁄₈"

Bottom

3¹⁄₈"

Inside

Fold into a triangle and sew

13³⁄₈"

15³⁄₈"

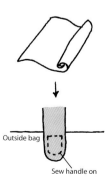

Outside bag

Sew handle on

Baby Booties ◑ ℂ

Photograph on pages 18–19.

Finished Size: 4″ long x 1⅜″ or ⅞″ tall x ⅝″ deep

Note: Use the same pattern paper for both the beige and the pink booties. The pattern is for slippers 4" long. The method for making a bag shape is shown on pages 48 to 49.

Materials for the Beige Booties

* Wool for the booties: Beige, 1½ ounces per bootie
* Wool for the felt balls: Moss green, yellow, or orange, small amounts of each

Materials for the Pink Booties

* Wool for the outside booties: Pink, ¾ ounce per bootie
* Wool for the lining: Natural, ¾ ounce per bootie
* Wool for the pom-pom: Natural, ¼ ounce

Instructions

1. Divide the wool for the bootie into eight equal parts. If making the pink bootie, divide the outside wool and the lining into four equal parts each.

2. Cut out a piece of pattern paper (see page 89). Felt four layers of wool on both sides of the pattern paper to make a bag shape. If making the pink bootie, work from the outside to the inside: first felt two layers of the pink wool for the outside, then the two layers of natural wool for the inside.

3. Referring to the diagram, cut an opening for the foot, remove the pattern paper, and turn the slipper right side out. Continue the felting process by rolling and rubbing the slipper surfaces until the slipper is near the desired size.

4. If making the pink bootie, cut away more of the opening to make it rounder. For both booties, insert your hand in the slipper and continue felting to raise the heel and toe parts until they are the size indicated in the diagram.

5. Rinse, spin, and then iron the bootie into shape. Let it dry naturally.

6. For the beige booties, make the felt balls following the instructions on page 54. For the pink booties, make the pom-pom following the instructions on page 76. Sew them onto the booties.

Step 3

Beige

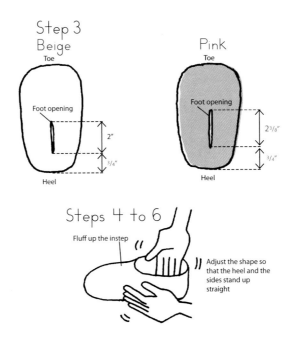

Toe

Foot opening

2"

3/4"

Heel

Pink

Toe

Foot opening

2 3/8"

3/4"

Heel

Steps 4 to 6

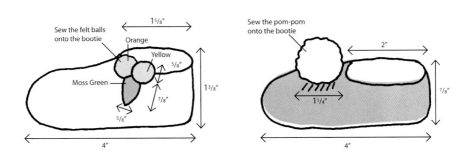

Fluff up the instep

Adjust the shape so that the heel and the sides stand up straight

Sew the felt balls onto the bootie

Orange

Yellow

Moss Green

1 5/8"

5/8"

7/8"

5/8"

1 3/8"

4"

Sew the pom-pom onto the bootie

2"

1 1/4"

7/8"

4"

Baby's Backpack

Photograph on pages 22–23.

Finished Size: 7⅞″ square

Materials

* Wool felt sheet for the main body: Lemon, 19¾" × 39⅜"
* Wool felt sheet for the stripes: Light blue and chartreuse, 9⅞" × 19¾"
* Yarn for stitching: Green, as needed
* One zipper: 5½" long
* Two leather cords: ¼" × 19¾"

Instructions

1. Cut the felt sheet for the main body of the backpack into eight 9⅞" squares.
2. Cut the felt sheet for the stripes into narrow strips, as you like.
3. Cut out a piece of pattern paper (see page 92). Cut the felt for the main body into the shape of the pattern. Working from the outside to the inside, felt four layers of felt sheets on both sides of the pattern paper to make a bag shape: first arrange the stripes on the paper, then felt the four layers of felt sheets on each side.
4. Referring to the diagram, cut an opening, and then remove the pattern paper and turn the backpack right side out. Continue the felting process by rolling and unrolling it from all sides until it has reached the size indicated in the diagram.
5. Rinse and spin, iron the backpack, and then let it dry naturally.
6. Machine sew the zipper into the opening. Hand sew running stitches with the yarn as you like. Cut holes for the leather straps, and insert the ends into the bag. Knot the ends of the strap to keep them in place.

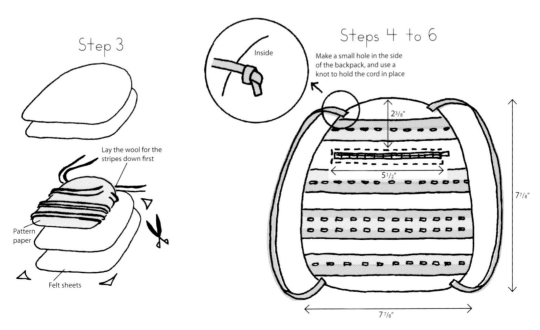

Step 3

Lay the wool for the stripes down first

Pattern paper

Felt sheets

Inside

Steps 4 to 6

Make a small hole in the side of the backpack, and use a knot to hold the cord in place

2⅜″

5½"

7⅞"

7⅞"

Clatter Balls

Photograph on page 24.

Finished Size: 2 1/8" in diameter

Note: The procedure for making this item is shown in the photographs on page 51.

Materials

* Wool for the ball: Dark red, indigo, or green, 3/4 ounce
* Sheet of wool felt for the shapes: Pink, light blue, or lemon, a small amount
* One plastic bell: 1" in diameter
* Yarn for stitching: White, about 11 7/8"

Instructions

1. Create a template of the pattern found on page 89. Cut the felt sheet for the pattern into heart shapes.
2. Wrap the wool for the ball around the plastic bell little by little. Apply a little hot, soapy water, and work it in gently.
3. When the ball gets larger, place it in a plastic bag and roll and rub it in the palm of your hand to felt it to the size shown in the diagram.
4. Place the decorative heart on the ball, and work it in thoroughly.
5. Rinse and spin the ball, and then let it dry naturally.
6. Stitch around the heart with yarn.

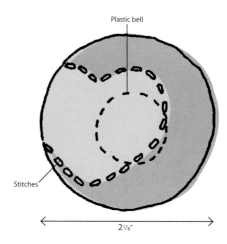

Plastic bell

Stitches

2 1/8"

Pastel-Colored Play Mat ⬤

Photograph on page 25.

Finished Size: 35 ½″ x 17 ¾″

Materials

* Sheet of wool felt for the mat: Natural, three sheets, 19¾″ × 39⅜″
* Sheet of wool felt for the rectangles and squares: Lemon, peach, light blue, pink, and blue, 1 piece each, 9⅞″ × 8⅝″

Instructions

1. Cut the felt sheets for the rectangles and squares: cut the peach, light blue, and pink pieces in two pieces each, and cut the rest into four pieces each.
2. Lay the three natural sheets of felt for the mat on top of each other. Arrange the decorative pieces on top of them as shown in the diagram. Apply hot, soapy water to the whole project, and gently work it in.
3. When the rectangles and squares are thoroughly embedded, continue to roll and rub the sheet until it reaches the size indicated in the diagram.
4. Cut the edges, and work them some more to make them straight.
5. Rinse, spin, and iron the mat, and then let it dry naturally.

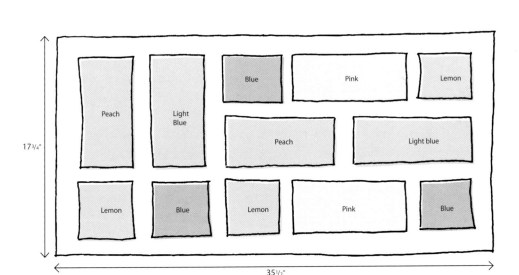

Soft Flower Vase ◑

Photograph on page 26.

Finished Size: 3 1/4″ high x 1 5/8″ in diameter

Materials

* Wool for the vase: Natural, camel, and brown (for the brown vase) or natural, gray, and dark gray (for the gray vase), less than 1/4 ounce each
* Glass bottle: 3 1/4" high × 1 5/8" in diameter

Instructions

1. Cover the opening of the bottle. Wrap the natural-colored wool around the entire glass bottle little by little. Apply hot, soapy water, and start felting. (If the bottle you are felting is larger or smaller than the one in the materials list, adjust the amount of wool accordingly.)
2. Wrap the bottom two-thirds of the bottle, half of it with light-colored wool and half with dark wool. Start felting it gently.

3. Put the covered bottle in a plastic bag, and roll and rub with the palm of your hand to continue felting it.
4. Cut away the opening, and felt the edge of the mouth to cover it.
5. Rinse the felted bottle, and then let it dry naturally.

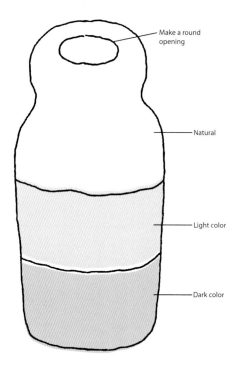

Make a round opening

Natural

Light color

Dark color

Polka Dot Hangers ◑ ⓡ

Photograph on page 27.

Finished Size: 9 ½″ wide

Materials

* Wool for the hanger cover: Natural, 1 ounce
* Wool for the polka dots: Camel, a small amount
* One metal hanger
* Linen ribbon: Beige, 1" × 39⅜"

Instructions

1. Bend the hanger into the shape shown in the diagram. (If it is too difficult to do by hand, use a small pair of pliers.) Wind the ribbon tightly around the hanger from the hook to the shoulders.
2. Wrap the natural-colored wool around the hanger, starting at one of the shoulders. Apply hot, soapy water, and gently work it in. Put the hanger inside a plastic bag, and push and rub it to continue the felting process until it is the size indicated in the drawing. (Take care not to get the hook wet.)
3. Rinse the hanger, iron it, and let it dry naturally.
4. Needle felt the polka dots onto the hanger.

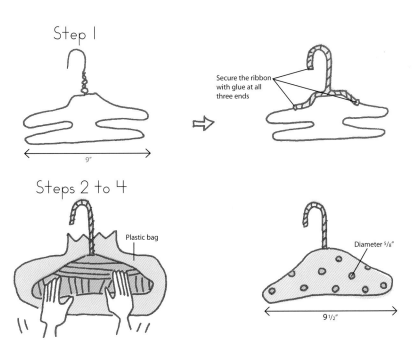

Step 1

9″

Secure the ribbon with glue at all three ends

Steps 2 to 4

Plastic bag

Diameter ⅝″

9 ½″

Elf Hat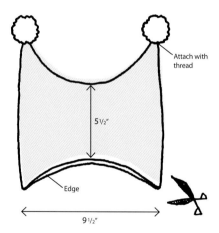

Photograph on page 28.

Finished Size: One size fits all

Note: The method for making a bag shape is shown on pages 48 to 49.

Materials

* Wool for the outside of the hat: Gray, 1 ounce
* Wool for the inside of the hat: Natural, 1 ounce
* Wool for the pom-poms: Natural, less than ½ ounce

Instructions

1. Divide the wool for the inside and outside of the hat into four equal parts each.
2. Cut out a piece of pattern paper (see page 89). Working from the outside to the inside, felt four layers of wool on both sides of the pattern paper to make a bag shape: first felt two layers of gray wool for the outside, then two layers of natural wool for the inside.
3. Cut an opening across the bottom, remove the pattern paper, and turn the hat inside out. Continue rolling the hat to felt it until it reaches the size indicated in the diagram.
4. Rinse, spin, and iron the hat, and then let it dry naturally.
5. Following the instructions in the sidebar below, make two pom-poms. Sew them to the hat.

Attach with thread

5½"

Edge

9½"

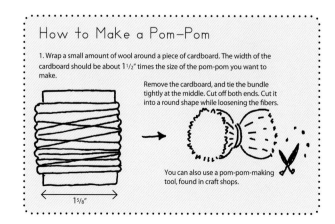

How to Make a Pom-Pom

1. Wrap a small amount of wool around a piece of cardboard. The width of the cardboard should be about 1½" times the size of the pom-pom you want to make.

Remove the cardboard, and tie the bundle tightly at the middle. Cut off both ends. Cut it into a round shape while loosening the fibers.

You can also use a pom-pom-making tool, found in craft shops.

1⅝"

Felt Ball Hair Tie 🄵

Photograph on page 29.

Materials

* Wool for the felt balls: Wine, brown, or natural, 1/16 ounce each
* One elastic hair tie: Brown, 1/8"

Instructions

1. Following the instructions on page 54, make two felt balls with 1/16 ounce of wool.
2. Sew the balls onto the hair tie.

Step 1

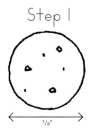

7/8"

Step 2

Sew on with thread

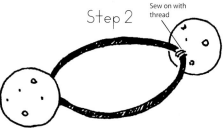

Wall Pockets ◑

Photograph on pages 30–31.

Finished Size: One size fits all

Materials

* Sheets of wool felt for the background: Blue, 2 pieces, 19³⁄₄" × 39³⁄₈"
* Sheets of wool felt for the stripes: Light blue and natural, 1 piece each, 19³⁄₄" × 39³⁄₈"
* Yarn or embroidery floss for stitching: Blue, 76³⁄₄" to 118"
* Wooden dowel: ³⁄₈" × 21¹⁄₂"
* Linen fabric: As needed

Instructions

1. Cut the felt sheets for the stripes into sixteen strips, each 1¹⁄₄" wide.
2. Place the two layers for the main sheet on top of each other. Then lay the stripes on top of the sheet, alternating the colors. Gently start the felting process by applying hot, soapy water to the whole project, and working it into the wool.
3. Once the pattern has been worked into the wool sheets, roll and rub the whole project to continue the felting process until it measures 17³⁄₄" × 35¹⁄₂".
4. Cut the edges, then work them some more to make sure they are straight.
5. Rinse, spin, and iron the sheet, and then let it dry naturally.
6. Fold the lower part of the wall pocket up about 6¹⁄₄" to create pockets. Mark the finished size of the wall pocket, and cut off the leftover fabric. Cut this extra fabric into a photo frame and small pockets, and sew them on.
7. Fold ⁷⁄₈" of the top of the wall pocket to the back, and sew it down. Pass the wooden dowel through the folded-over part. (You may want attach linen tabs to the dowel or wall pocket, depending on where you hang it.)

Step 2

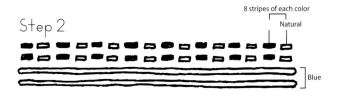

8 stripes of each color

Natural

Blue

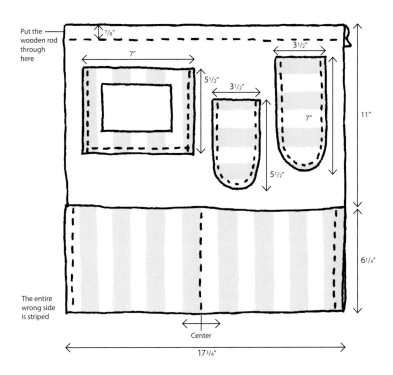

Put the wooden rod through here

7/8"

7"

5½"

3½"

3½"

3½"

7"

11"

5½"

6¼"

The entire wrong side is striped

Center

17¾"

Bluebird Mobile 🍓

Photograph on pages 32–33.

Finished Size: 9 ½" wide

Materials

* Wool for the bird bodies: Light blue, navy blue, lavender, and purple
* Wool for the eyes: White, a small amount
* Wool for the pupils: Black, a small amount
* Wool for the beak: Yellow, a small amount
* Wool for the felt balls: Small amounts in the four colors of the birds and in white
* Two wooden dowels: $1/4$" × $7 7/8$" each
* Linen cord: $59 1/8$"
* Yarn: White, 71"
* Two wooden beads: Brown, $1/4$" in diameter

Instructions

1. Starting with a small amount of wool, and referring to the instructions on page 54, make one bird in each of the four colors to the size indicated in the diagram. Make the wings, and attach the fluffy ends to the bird body. Needle felt the eyes and tail stripes.
2. Following the directions on page 54, make 18 felt balls in three different sizes and five different colors.
3. Drill holes in the wooden dowels, and pass the linen cord through the holes at the midpoint.
4. Using a large sewing needle, pass the linen cord through the birds and felt balls. Hang them on the wooden rods as shown in the diagram. Carefully balance the number and weight of the felt balls, birds, and cord so that the wooden dowels remain horizontal.

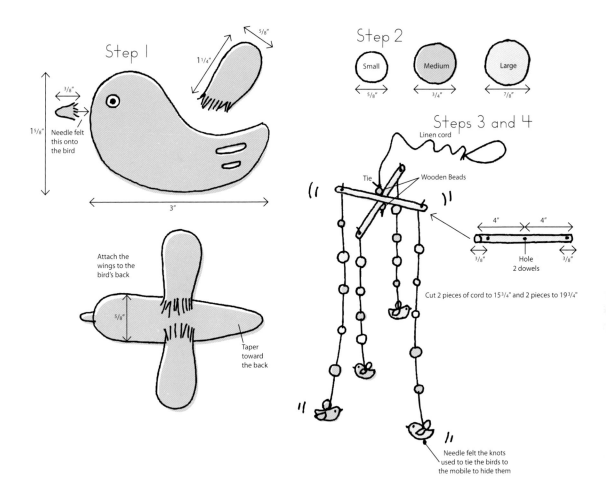

Step 1

5/8"

1 1/4"

3/8"

Needle felt this onto the bird

1 5/8"

3"

Attach the wings to the bird's back

5/8"

Taper toward the back

Step 2

Small   Medium   Large

5/8"   3/4"   7/8"

Steps 3 and 4

Linen cord

Tie   Wooden Beads

4"   4"

Hole
2 dowels

3/8"   3/8"

Cut 2 pieces of cord to 15 3/4" and 2 pieces to 19 3/4"

Needle felt the knots used to tie the birds to the mobile to hide them

Mini Cushions ⊕

Photograph on page 34.

Finished Size: 7⅞" square

Materials

* Sheet of wool felt for the cushion: Beige, 19¾" × 39⅜"
* Sheets of wool felt for the pattern: Camel and brown (for the brown cushion) or gray and dark gray (for the gray cushion), 1 piece each, 9⅞" × 8⅝"
* Cotton batting: As needed

Instructions

1. Cut the felt sheet for the cushion into four pieces, 19¾" × 9⅞" each
2. Cut a total of eight circles out of the felt sheets: two each of two different sizes in both colors.
3. Cut out a piece of pattern paper 9" square (see page 91). Cut notches into one of the felt sheets for the main cushion. Arrange the decorative circles on the surface. Sprinkle hot, soapy water, and gently felt the entire surface to secure the shapes. Place the pattern sheet on the side with the notches, and fold the edges over the paper. Fold the entire cushion in half over the paper. Cut off any felt that sticks out. Continue wet felting around the entire cushion surface.
4. Cut notches in the other three sheets of the felt for the cushion. Place the cushion on the second layer of felt. Fold over the notches, then fold layer 2 in half. Continue felting and adding layers 3 and 4. Alternate the side on which the fold is placed and the surface on which the notched tabs are folded, making sure that the thickness of the folded part is uniform on both surfaces and around all four sides.
5. Cut an opening about 2¾" along one edge, remove the pattern paper, and turn the cushion right side out. Continue rolling and working the felt until it is a uniform 7⅞" square.
6. Rinse, spin, and iron the cushion, and then let it dry naturally.
7. Stuff the pillow through the opening with cotton batting. Hand sew the opening shut. Take the pieces that were cut off in step 3, and needle felt them over the seam, hiding the stitches.

Step 2

Large

3"

Small

2³/₄"

Step 3

First layer

Decorative pattern

Notches →

Tabs →

9"

Pattern paper

9"

Arrange the decorative pattern under the pattern paper, too

Cut the corners off

Fold

Fold up and over →

Pattern paper

Fold

Surface A

Cut off anything that sticks out

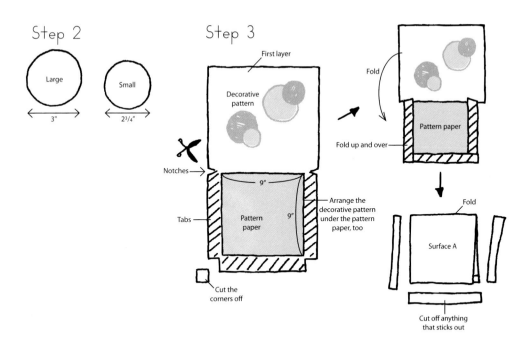

Step 4

With each layer, move the position of the fold over

1st layer
2nd layer

Surface B
Fold

Fold

3rd layer
4th layer

Each time you felt a layer around the paper, turn it over (surface A to surface B)

Step 7

Cotton batting

Cut opening

7⁷/₈"

Pattern paper

1st layer
2nd layer
3rd layer

4th layer

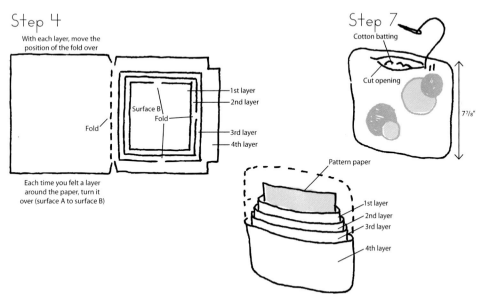

Fragrant Sachets ❶ ❷

Photograph on page 35.

Finished Size: Shoe, 11″ wide x 3½″ tall x ⅞″ deep; Shirt, 4⅜″ wide x 5½″ tall x ⅞″ deep

Note: The method for making a bag shape is shown on pages 48 to 49.

Materials

* Wool for the shirt: Beige, ¾ ounce
* Wool for the shirt bottom: Yellow, a small amount
* Wool for the shoe: Beige, ½ ounce
* Wool for the shoe opening: Light blue, a small amount
* Cotton batting: As needed
* Dried herbs: As needed
* Suede cord: 7⅞"
* Yarn for stitching: Orange for the T-shirt and blue for the shoe, about 11⅞"

Instructions

1. Divide the beige wool for the main item into eight equal parts.
2. Cut out a piece of pattern paper (see page 90). Felt four layers of wool on both sides of the pattern paper to make a bag shape.
3. If you're making the T-shirt, cut an opening at the bottom. If you're making the shoe, cut an opening across the top. Remove the pattern paper, and turn the item right side out. Continue the felting process by rolling and rubbing the item until it is the size indicated in the diagram.
4. Rinse, spin, and iron the item, and then let it dry naturally.
5. Insert the cotton batting and dried herbs. Needle felt the contrasting wool for the bottom opening of the T-shirt or the top opening of the shoe to close the opening.
6. Hand stitch the yarn to simulate ties. Add a piece of suede cord to hang it.

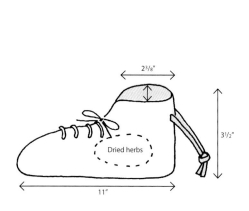

2³⁄₈"

3½"

Dried herbs

11"

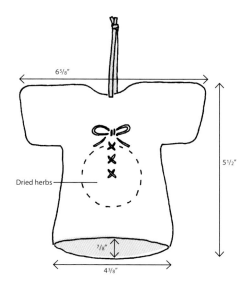

6⁵⁄₈"

5½"

Dried herbs

⅞"

4³⁄₈"

Mushroom Box ◖ ⌔

Photograph on page 36.

Finished Size: About 4 1/8″ in diameter × 3 1/2″ tall

Note: The method for making a bag shape is shown on pages 48 to 49.

Materials

* Wool for the container: Natural, 1/2 ounce
* Wool for the lid: Brown, 1 ounce
* Wool for the polka dots: Natural, a small amount

Instructions

1. Divide the wool for the container into eight equal parts.

2. Cut out a piece of pattern paper (see page 92). Felt four layers of wool on both sides of the pattern paper to make a bag shape.

3. Cut an opening across top, remove the pattern paper, and turn the item right side out. Continue the felting process by rolling and rubbing. Shape the bottom and sides using an existing container. Work around the top edge to ensure an even height as you felt the item to the size indicated in the diagrams.

4. Rinse, spin, and iron the container, and let it dry naturally.

5. Needle felt about 1/2 ounce of the brown wool for the lid into a hill shape, and then work in the dots.

6. Add the remaining brown wool to the underside of the lid, and needle felt it until it is the shape shown in the diagram.

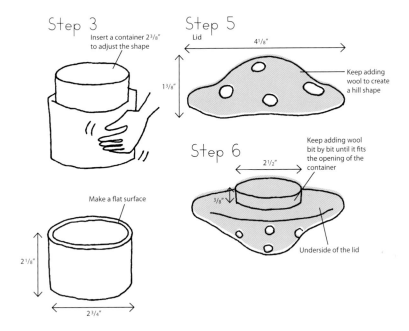

Step 3
Insert a container 2 3/8″ to adjust the shape
1 3/8″
Make a flat surface
2 1/8″
2 3/4″

Step 5
Lid
4 1/8″
Keep adding wool to create a hill shape

Step 6
2 1/2″
3/8″
Keep adding wool bit by bit until it fits the opening of the container
Underside of the lid

Baby Bottle Holder ●

Photograph on page 37.

Finished Size: About 10˝ tall × 2¾˝ in diameter

Note: The method for making a bag shape is shown on pages 48 to 49.

Materials

* Wool for the container: Natural, 1 ounce
* Wool for the shapes: Gray, ⅛ ounce
* Linen for the top: Beige, 5¾" × 5⅞"
* Two suede cords: 19¾" each

Instructions

1. Divide the wool for the container into eight equal parts.
2. Cut out a piece of pattern paper (see page 92). Working from the outside to the inside, felt four layers of wool on both sides of the pattern paper to make a bag shape: first arrange the shapes on the paper, then felt four layers of wool.
3. Cut an opening across the top, remove the pattern paper, and turn the container right side out. Continue the felting process by rolling and rubbing the item.
4. Continue felting to make a three-dimensional cylinder. Shape the bottom and sides using an existing container.
5. Rinse, spin, and iron the container, and then let it dry naturally.
6. Hem the four sides of the linen. Place the linen over the edge of the container, and sew it in place. Hand stitch the open sides of the linen together. Sew around the top of the linen, forming a casing for the cords. Insert the cords, and tie the ends.

Step 4

Insert a container about 2 3/8" in diameter to adjust the shape

Step 6

Fabric around the opening

5/8" seam allowance

4 1/2"

Fold over twice and machine stitch

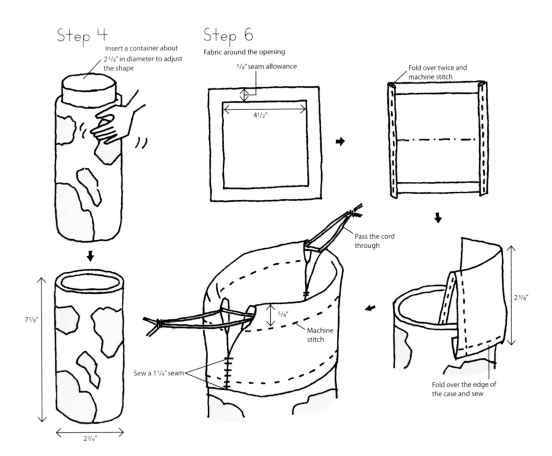

Pass the cord through

Machine stitch

5/8"

Sew a 1 1/4" seam

7 7/8"

2 3/4"

2 5/8"

Fold over the edge of the case and sew

Teddy Bear ⓡ

Photograph on pages 38–39.

Finished Size: 15⅜″ tall and
10¼″ in diameter

Materials

* Wool for the bear: Camel, 5¼ ounces
* Two glass eyes: ¼″ in diameter
* Embroidery floss: Black, as needed

Instructions

1. Needle felt the head, trunk, limbs, and ears separately. Join the pieces together. Consult the diagram and photographs as you shape the face and plump out the torso. Note: You can work more efficiently on large projects if you use a felting needle with three to six points.
2. Attach the glass eyes, and embroider the mouth and nose.

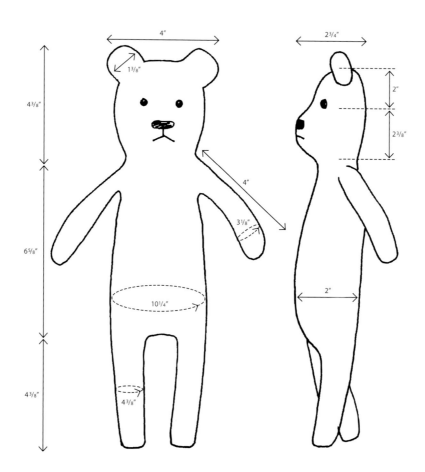

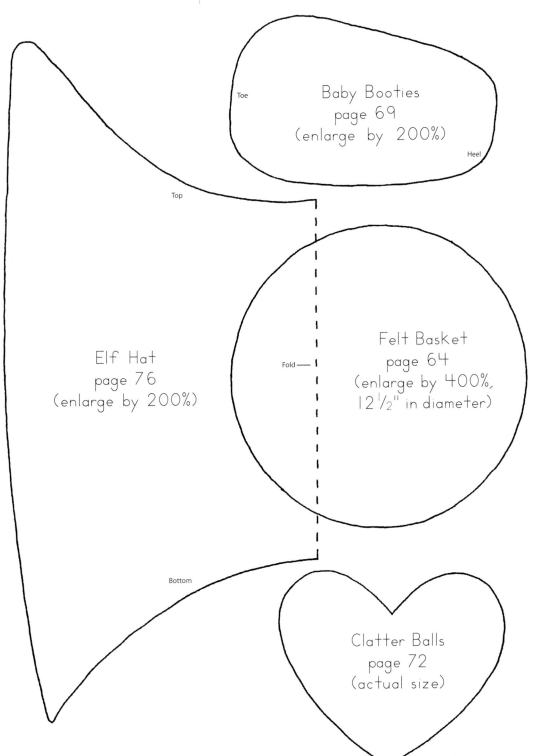

Baby Booties
page 69
(enlarge by 200%)

Toe

Heel

Top

Elf Hat
page 76
(enlarge by 200%)

Fold —

Felt Basket
page 64
(enlarge by 400%,
12 1/2" in diameter)

Bottom

Clatter Balls
page 72
(actual size)

Mama's Bag page 68
(enlarge by 200%, 17 3/4" x 15 3/4")

Fragrant Sachets:
T-shirt
page 84
(enlarge by 200%)

Fragrant Sachets: Shoes
page 84
(enlarge by 200%)

Lamb Place Mat
and Coasters
page 65
(actual size)

Large Flower Pattern
page 66
(enlarge by 200%)

Small Flower Pattern
Page 66
(enlarge by 200%)

Top

Warm Vest
page 62
(enlarge by 200%, 13 3/8" × 14 1/2")

Top

Four-Leaf Clover Notebook Holder
page 61
(enlarge by 200%, 9" × 12 1/2")

Mini Cushions
page 82
(enlarge by 200%)

Gingerbread Man Puppets
page 63
(enlarge by 200%)

Clover Pattern
page 53 and 61 (actual size)

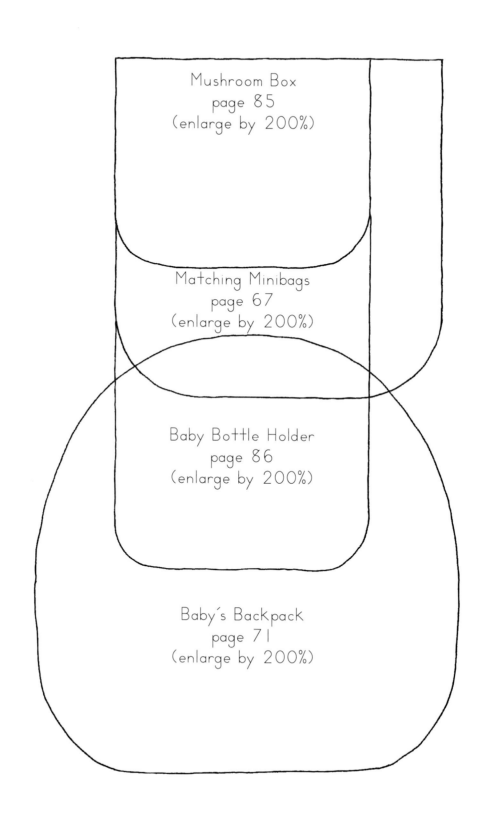

Mushroom Box
page 85
(enlarge by 200%)

Matching Minibags
page 67
(enlarge by 200%)

Baby Bottle Holder
page 86
(enlarge by 200%)

Baby's Backpack
page 71
(enlarge by 200%)

Techniques and Terminology

This list explains the main techniques and terminology for felt work. You will find it useful when you are puzzled about how to proceed or when you want to try new arrangements.

Color blending: A technique for blending wool colors. You can use specialized tools, or unravel the fibers with your finger tip to blend them.

Core: Wrap layers of wool around a core in order to make a stable, solid object.

Corriedale: A breed of sheep with wool of uniform thickness and sturdiness that has found a wide range of uses.

Cuticle: An extremely fine, thin layer on the surface of raw wool fibers. Felting occurs when the cuticles become entwined and tangled with one another.

Dividing: Dividing skeins of wool into the number of parts needed for a specific project.

Dividing equally: In order to arrange wool correctly, it is necessary to measure the whole quantity accurately and divide it into equal parts.

Felt ball: A ball of wool that has been felted.

Felting: A process that uses jabs with a needle, heat, vibration, or friction to entangle and shrink wool fibers.

Felting needle: A special needle for felt work. Some types have between three and six pins.

Fleece: Raw wool that is completely unprocessed.

Horizontal alignment: Arranging strands of wool so that they are arrayed horizontally from your point of view.

Hot, soapy water: A mixture of a small amount of liquid detergent in a large amount of hot water. The alkali contained in the detergent facilitates the felting process in so-called wet felting.

Layers of wool: In this book, this indicates the way wool is arranged and laid out before felting. For example: "Divide wool into six equal portions, lay the fibers out in alternating horizontal and vertical layers, and felt them" or "Arrange four layers on each side and felt them into a bag shape."

Making a bag shape: Felting wool to envelope a piece of pattern paper, and pulling out the paper to make a hollow object. If you cut an opening, you can make a bag.

Making a sheet: The act of making a flat felted surface out of raw wool.

Making three-dimensional objects: Making bags or containers out of felt by raising and felting the sides and shaping it with a mold, or simply rubbing it by hand.

Merino: A breed of sheep. Since this wool has soft and thin fibers, it is often used for mufflers and other items that touch the skin.

Needle: In this book, it refers to a felting needle.

Needle felting: A technique for felting that involves poking wool with a needle until it reaches the desired hardness. It can be used to make all kinds of shapes, depending on the position and direction that one pokes.

Needling: A technique for attaching wool and felted pieces to each other by poking them with a needle.

Pinch Test: A test for checking the completeness of a felting project. (See page 49).

Pom-pom: A technique that involves bundling wool, cutting it to uniform lengths, and trimming it into a ball shape.

Raw wool: Wool from sheep, the raw material for felt, wool yarn, and woven wool cloth. Depending on how and whether it is washed and/or carded, the wool is classified under such names as "roving" or "sliver."

Removing pattern paper: When you are felting a bag-shaped item, you cut the felted wool open and remove the pattern paper so that the inside is hollow.

Rolling up: One of the methods for felting, it involves rolling up a sheet of felt on a rod and pressing it firmly.

Sliver: Freshly shorn wool that is carded by machine, cleaned, and made uniform by removing its short, stray hairs, so that its fibers are long and straight.

Spin drying: This stage of finishing wet felted fabric involves removing excess water by running the fabric through the spin cycle in a washing machine.

Stripes: A pattern made by laying strands of two or more different colors alongside one another.

Turn right side out: A necessary step after you have felted the inside and outside of a bag-shaped item.

Vertical alignment: Arranging strands of wool so that they are arrayed vertically from your point of view.

Wet felting: A technique for making felt using liquid detergent and hot water.

Working in: This felting techniques involves rubbing and stroking the fibers to entwine with one another.

Wrapping pattern paper: Placing pattern paper between the two sides of a bag-shaped item as you add layers to it and join the edges.

About the Author

SAORI YAMAZAKI has enjoyed making handcrafts since she was a little girl. Since 2001, she has been well known for her handmade felt items, which have been featured in magazines and on television. These days, she especially enjoys meeting people face to face at workshops and exhibitions. She announces and sells her work on her Web site, atelier Charmy's (www.atelier-charmys.com), where her best-selling item is a made-to-order felt dog. She shares her home and life with three dogs, Charmy, Beau, and Mametaro. She lives in Tokyo.

Special thanks to Ryo Miyashita

TRUMPETER BOOKS
An imprint of Shambhala Publications, Inc.
Horticultural Hall
300 Massachusetts Avenue
Boston, Massachusetts 02115
www.shambhala.com

9 8 7 6 5 4 3 2 1

First English Edition
Printed in China

⊗ This edition is printed on acid-free paper that meets the
American National Standards Institute z39.48 Standard.
♻ Shambhala Publications makes every effort to print on recycled paper.
For more information please visit www.shambhala.com.

Distributed in the United States by Random House, Inc.,
and in Canada by Random House of Canada Ltd

Designed by Daniel Urban-Brown

Library of Congress Cataloging-in-Publication Data
Yamazaki, Saori.
Felting for baby: 25 warm and woolly projects for the little ones in your life / Saori Yamazaki.
     p. cm.
ISBN 978-1-59030-716-8 (pbk.: alk. paper)
1. Felt work. 2. Infants' supplies. 1. Title.
TT849.5.Y3612 2009
746'.0463—dc22
2009010426